THINK and SOLVE

2

HAROLD CLARKE
ROBERT SHEPHERD

CAMBRIDGE
UNIVERSITY PRESS

Designed and illustrated by Celia Hart
Cover design by Chris McLeod

PUBLISHED BY THE PRESS SYNDICATE OF THE UNIVERSITY OF CAMBRIDGE
The Pitt Building, Trumpington Street, Cambridge CB2 1RP, United Kingdom

CAMBRIDGE UNIVERSITY PRESS
The Edinburgh Building, Cambridge CB2 2RU, United Kingdom
40 West 20th Street, New York, NY 10011–4211, USA
10 Stamford Road, Oakleigh, Melbourne 3166, Australia

First published 1984
Eleventh printing 1997

Printed in the United Kingdom at the University Press, Cambridge

ISBN 0 521 26972 5

Task 1

1 What is five more than 16?

2 Take nine from 22.

3 If balloons cost 7p, how much will 4 cost?

4 How many balloons can I buy with 35p?

5 Philip has 6 conkers, and Pam has twelve.
How many have they altogether?

6 What is one more than 149?

7 Write the largest and smallest numbers
in this list: 87, 79, 76, 93, 80.

8 Add 10 to 121.

9 How far away from the nearest ten is 83?

10 Write **one hundred and seven** in figures.

11 What is half of 28?

12 Does this clock say 12:20?

13 Is 115 > 112?

> 4 > 3 means
> 4 is bigger than 3

14 Do we measure the height of girls
in kilograms or in centimetres?

15 What is the next number? 12, 15, 18, ?

16 What number when multiplied by 4 gives the answer 24?

17 Rosie's cat weighs 3 kilograms. Her dog weighs
11 kilograms more. How heavy is her dog?

18 The bus should have left at 5 minutes past 6, but
was ten minutes late. When did it leave?

19 Add together the odd numbers between 12 and 16.

20 In my garden I have 30 roses. Ten are red,
15 are yellow and the rest are white. How many are white?

Task 2

1 Add together seven and 22.

2 From nineteen take 8.

3 If a packet has 6 pencils in it,
how many pencils are there in 5 packets?

4 John has 28p. If he spends 9p, how much has he left?

5 Share 36 by 4.

6 Write **142** in words.

7 What is the value of the six in 163?

8 Write the smallest and largest numbers
in this list: 24, 33, 30, 42, 27.

9 14×10.

10 Take 10 from 137.

11 Is sugar weighed in grams or in metres?

12 How many days are there in December?

13 Is $12 > 3 \times 3$?

14 Is this shape
a triangle?

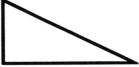

15 How many weeks are there in a year?

16 Apples cost 7p, and oranges 8p.
How much would 2 apples and 3 oranges cost?

17 There are 6 rows of four eggs, but three eggs
are broken. How many whole eggs are there?

18 How many children are there in a class of
16 boys and 18 girls?

19 3 boys and 2 girls have each collected ten stamps.
How many stamps have they collected altogether?

20 If I save 5p a day for a week,
how much will I have saved?

Task 3

A

1   Add eight to 33.

2   23 − 7.

3   Multiply 5 by 9.

4   Jill has eighteen sweets. She eats seven of them.
    How many are left?

5   Share 32 by 4.

6   16 × 10.

7   What number is one more than 169?

8   Take 10 from 173.

9   Write the smallest and largest numbers
    in this list: 57,   35,   37,   53,   44.

10 Write **128** in words.

B

11 What is double 12?

12 How many minutes are there in ¾ of an hour?

13 Does this clock
    say 7:20?

14 Is 15 > 4 × 4?

15 Do we measure the distance between towns in
    litres or in kilometres?

16 Packets of chewing gum cost 7p.
    How many packets can I buy with 42p?

17 I have saved four 1p coins, three 2p coins and
    one 5p coin. How much have I?

18 When I have gone 4 kilometres, I have done
    half of my journey. How far is it altogether?

19 There were 20 people on a bus. 5 got on and 10 got
    off. How many were on the bus now?

20 Alice is 11 years old. Ben is three years younger.
    How old is Ben?

Snakes and ladders

Each snake has a number pattern.
Write the pattern and fill in the missing numbers.
Add the numbers on the ladders and find the total for
each one.

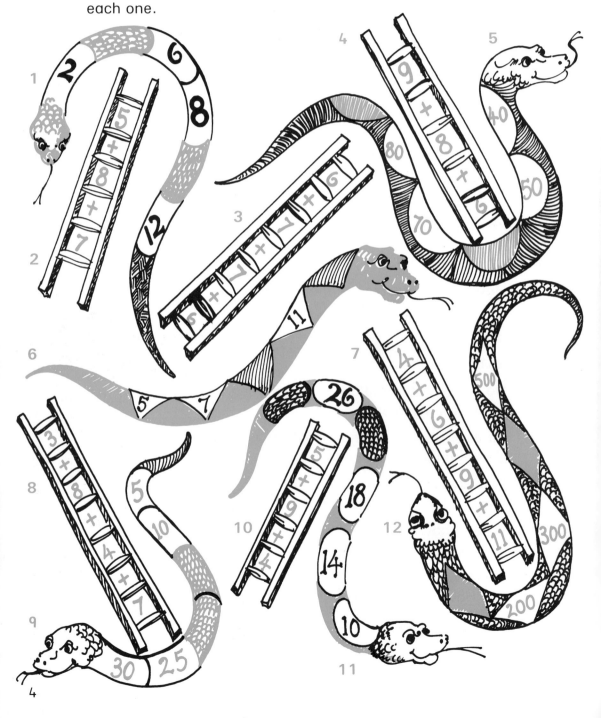

4

Task 4

1 What is the total of nine and 24?

2 What is six less than 32?

3 8 × 4.

4 How many pairs can I make from 16 matching blue socks?

5 Jim needs 14p more to buy a 40p ball.
How much has he now?

6 What is the value of the seven in 172?

7 Write in figures. **one hundred and seventy-five**.

8 How far away from the nearest ten is 87?

9 Write the smallest and largest numbers in this list:
42, 33, 24, 34, 43.

10 23 × 10.

11 How many days are there in January?

12 Is 7 a multiple of 2?

13 Is this
an equilateral triangle?

> These are multiples of 2:
> 2, 4, 6, 8, 10
> 12
> 14
> 16
> 18
> and on and on

14 What is the next number?   13,   15,   17,   19,   ?

15 Do we measure petrol in litres or in centimetres?

16 If I save 20p a day from Sunday until the next
Thursday, how much will I have?

17 Bananas cost 8p each, and pears cost 9p.
How much would a banana and 2 pears cost?

18 I was 15 minutes early for the half past three train.
When did I arrive?

19 What number multiplied by three gives the answer 21?

20 I had 40 books. I sold 15 and gave away 10.
How many did I have left?

Task 5

1 What is nine more than 32?

2 Take eight from 34.

3 What are 7 lots of 7?

4 Megan, Tim and Harold share 27 marbles.
   How many do they each get?

5 Pat and David share 48 conkers. How many do they
   each get?

6 How far from the nearest ten is 48?

7 240 ÷ 10.

8 Put these in order, smallest first: 79,   62,   90.

9 What number is one more than 159?

10 Write **133** in words.

11 If today is Monday, what day will it be in nine days' time?

12 Is half of 20 < 2 × 6?

> 4 < 6
> means 4 is less than 6

13 Which four coins make 37p?

14 A quarter past three is the same as 3:15. True or false?

15 Are ribbons measured in litres or in centimetres?

16 Gerry is 9 years old. Ellen was born five years before Gerry.
    How old is Ellen?

17 Add the even numbers between 15 and 21.

18 4 boys and 2 girls have each collected 4 conkers.
    How many have they altogether?

19 I have saved three 1p coins, two 2p coins and
    two 10p coins. How much have I saved altogether?

20 I have spent half of my pocket money, and have
    15p left. How much pocket money do I get?

A

1 Add 36 to seven.

2 29 − 17.

3 Candy bars cost 9p each. How much will 5 cost?

4 How many teams of four can I make from 36 children?

5 Share 21 by 7.

6 Write these in order, smallest first: 42, 37, 49.

7 170 ÷ 10.

8 Which two of these numbers add up to ten?
7, 6, 3, 2, 5.

9 Add ten to 143.

10 What is the largest number that can be made from these figures?

B

11 Does this clock read 6:45?

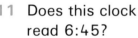

12 What is the next number? 12, 16, 20, 24, ?

13 Half past six is the same as 6:35. True or false?

14 Is 4 + 4 < 9 − 2?

15 How many corners are there on a cube?

16 Lollies cost 8p each. How many can I buy with 40p?

17 Oranges cost 7p each, and pears cost 6p.
How much do 2 oranges and 3 pears cost?

18 Pauline is two years older than Jeff.
Jeff is 13 years old. How old is Pauline?

19 What number multiplied by five gives the answer 25?

20 My bag weighs 4 kilograms and Dad's weighs 7 kilograms more. How heavy is Dad's bag?

Task 7

1 Find the sum of nine and thirty-seven.

2 What is six less than thirty-five?

3 Multiply eight by five.

4 Pears cost 9p each. How much will 4 pears cost?

5 How many pears can I buy with 45p?

6 Multiply 37 by 10.

7 How far from the nearest ten is 58?

8 Add 10 to 125.

9 Put these numbers in order, largest first: 41, 54, 37, 49.

10 Write **one hundred and sixty** in figures.

11 Do we weigh boys in kilograms or in kilometres?

12 What is double fifteen?

13 How many days are there in March?

14 Is 12 a multiple of 2?

15 Is 3:45 the same as a quarter to four?

16 Sheila is hiking. She has gone 7 kilometres and she is half-way. How long is her journey altogether?

17 If I save 10p a day from Saturday until the next Wednesday, how much will I have saved altogether?

18 How many children are there in a class of 16 boys and 17 girls?

19 There are seven rows of oranges with five in each row, but eight of them are bad. How many good oranges are there?

20 There were 30 people on a bus. 10 got on, and 5 got off. How many were on the bus now?

Starters

In each row start with the one on the left.
Put the next four items in the right order.
Use the letters A, B, C and D for each answer.

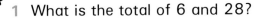

Task 8

A

1 What is the total of 6 and 28?

2 Take 4 from 21.

3 Pencils cost 7p each. How much will six pencils cost?

4 Share 30 by 6.

5 Mrs Roy owned 24 cows, but she sold seven at the market. How many had she left?

6 Write these in order, smallest first: 47, 35, 45, 39.

7 Which two of these numbers add up to ten?
5, 4, 7, 2, 6.

8 49×10.

9 What is the value of the one in 109?

10 What is the smallest number that can be made from these figures? **4 9 2**

B

11 Twenty minutes to six is the same as 6:20. True or false?

12 If today is Wednesday, which day will it be in 5 days' time?

13 How many days are there in September?

14 Is 22 a multiple of 2?

15 Do we measure the length of a garden in kilograms or in metres?

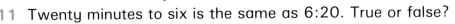

8 9 10 11 12 13 14

↑

halfway

16 What number is halfway between 9 and 13?

17 A train should have arrived at 4:15, but it was 15 minutes late. When did it arrive?

18 I bought two 6p biscuits.
What change did I get from 20p?

19 There are 32 children in a class.
18 of them are boys. How many girls are there?

20 I have saved three 1p coins, two 5p coins and two 10p coins. How much have I saved altogether?

1 Add together 7 and 24.

2 27 − 9.

3 Five girls are needed for a team.
How many girls are needed for 7 teams?

4 Divide 27 by 3.

5 Norma is making 4 trays of cakes. Each tray holds 9 cakes. How many cakes is Norma making altogether?

6 What number is ten less than 114?

7 Write **109** in words.

8 How far from the nearest 10 is 78?

9 32×10.

10 What is the smallest number in this list?
39, 42, 36, 63, 49.

11 What is a quarter of 40?

12 Which four coins make 46p?

13 What is the next number? 19, 17, 15, ?

14 Is 18 a multiple of 3?

15 Is sugar sold in kilograms or in kilometres?

16 Choc-drops are three for 5p.
How many will I get for 10p?

17 If I collect five-pence a day from Tuesday until Friday, how much will I have collected?

18 What number when multiplied by three gives the answer 24?

19 There were 10 people on a bus. 6 got on and 9 got off. How many were on the bus now?

20 My shopping weighs 6 kilograms, and Mum's weighs 9 kilograms more. How heavy is Mum's shopping?

$\frac{1}{4}$ of 40

Task 10

A

1 Add sixteen to eleven.

2 Take 13 from 24.

3 Tom, Dave and Martin each have nine marbles. How many do they have altogether?

4 Granny gets two bunches of flowers for her birthday. Each bunch has 12 flowers in it. How many flowers does she get altogether?

5 Share 20 by 4.

6 What is the largest number that can be made from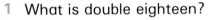

7 What is ten more than 123?

8 Write **one hundred and fifty-nine** in figures.

9 Which two of these numbers add up to ten? 3, 4, 2, 8, 9.

10 270 ÷ 10.

B

11 What is double eighteen?

12 Is 60 centimetres + 60 centimetres longer than a metre?

> 1 metre = 100 centimetres

13 What is the next number? 4, 7, 10, 13, ?

14 Is a quarter to seven the same as 6:45?

15 Is 14 a multiple of 3?

16 A lorry is carrying sacks of potatoes. It has three rows of sacks with 7 in each row. How many sacks are there altogether?

17 What number is halfway between 16 and 20?

> 16, 17, 18, 19, 20

18 There are six pairs of blue socks in a bag, but five socks have holes in them. How many socks do not need mending?

19 Apples cost 7p each and pears cost 9p. How much do two apples and two pears cost?

20 Mary is cycling and has gone half of the way. If she has gone nine kilometres, how far is the ride altogether?

More or less

Find out what these weigh together:

1 Cheese and tea.

2 Cornflakes and biscuits.

3 Two packets of butter and one packet of tea.

4 Three packets of tea.

5 Biscuits and butter.

6 Cornflakes and butter.

7 How much less than butter does tea weigh?

8 How much more than the biscuits does the cheese weigh?

9 What do biscuits, tea and butter weigh altogether?

10 Which weighs more, cheese and butter or biscuits and cornflakes?

Task 11

1 What is seven more than 29?

2 From sixteen take nine.

3 Neil is collecting 5p coins. He has eight of them so far.
   How much money is that altogether?

4 14 people each carry two suitcases into a hotel.
   How many cases is that altogether?

5 Share 24 marbles among three children.
   How many will they each get?

6 Write **one hundred and ninety-two** in figures.

7 How far from the nearest ten is 42?

8 What is ten less than 173?

9 What is the largest number that can be made from

10 Put these in order, largest first: 93,   89,   92,   79.

11 How many days are there in October?

12 If today is Sunday, what day will it be in 4 days' time?

13 Is 21 a multiple of three?

14 Is petrol bought in litres or in kilograms?

15 What is the next number?   18,   16,   14,   ?

16 I have 50p. I buy a book for 30p and some sweets
    for 12p. How much have I left?

17 I get 30p pocket money and have spent half of it.
    How much is left ?

18 If I collect ten-pence a day from Monday until
    Saturday, how much will I have?

19 What number when multiplied by 6 gives the answer 6?

20 The bus was ten minutes early. It should have
    arrived at 2:20. When did it arrive?

Task 12

A

1. Add twelve to sixteen.

2. 31 − 12.

3. Sue, Sarah, Dick and Dan each have six toy cars. How many do they have altogether?

4. Heather had 32p. She gave Jim 9p. How much did she have now?

5. Divide 33 by 3.

6. Put these in order, smallest first: 93, 82, 79, 88.

7. 190 ÷ 10.

8. What is the value of the seven in 179?

9. Which two of these numbers add up to ten? 4, 9, 3, 8, 1.

10. What number is ten more than 93?

B

11. Thirty-five minutes past six is the same as twenty-five minutes to seven. True or false?

12. What is a quarter of 16?

13. If today is Monday, what day was it three days ago?

14. Is 23 a multiple of three?

15. Are the lines in your books measured in centimetres or in metres?

> Multiples of three
> 3, 6, 9, 12, 15, 18
> 21...

16. If there are 28 children in a class and 12 of them are girls, how many boys are there?

17. Jane was born 5 years before Chris. Chris is 14 years old. How old is Jane?

18. Choc-dips cost 4 for 6p. How many can I get for 18p?

19. I have saved four 2p coins, three 5p coins and two 10p coins. How much have I saved?

20. There were 20 people on the bus. 6 got on, but 4 got off. How many were on the bus now?

15

Task 13

A

1 Add together twenty-five and six.

2 What is seventeen take away eight?

3 Multiply 7 by 8.

4 Share 28 conkers among four girls.
How many do they each get?

5 Arthur had 40p, but he then spent 9p. How much
had he left?

6 What is the value of the six in 160?

7 Which two of these numbers add up to ten?
7, 6, 2, 9, 3.

8 What is the largest number that can be made from

9 43×10.

10 What number is one less than 120?

B

11 How many grams are there in half a kilogram?

12 What is the next number?   4,   9,   14,   ?

13 Is $3 \times 10 < 4 + 10$?

1000 grams = 1 kilogram

14 How many days are there in August?

15 Is young Lucy 90 centimetres or 90 metres tall?

16 Oranges cost 9p each, and apples cost 8p.
How much would two oranges and three apples cost?

17 What number when multiplied by eight gives
24 as the answer?

18 Add the odd numbers between 8 and 14.

19 The train was ten minutes late. It should have
arrived at 2:15. When did it arrive?

20 Jason has spent half of his pocket money, and
has 75p left. How much pocket money does he get?

Task 14

1 Add twenty-five and nine.

2 24 − 6.

3 There are six tulips in a bunch.
How many tulips are there in 8 bunches?

4 How many pairs can be made from 34 children?

5 Billy has 44 marbles.
If he wins seven more, how many will he have?

6 Add 10 to 197.

7 How many tens are there in 270?

8 Write **408** in words.

9 Put these in order, largest first: 76,   92,   88,   86.

10 How far from the nearest ten is 76?

11 Is 34 a multiple of 4?

12 What is double seventeen?

13 How many days are there in five weeks?

14 If today is Wednesday, which day will it be
in eight days' time?

15 Does David weigh 50 grams or 50 kilograms?

16 What number is halfway between 24 and 30?

17 There are five teams of five children.
Nine of the children are boys. How many girls are there?

18 Which number when multiplied by 7 gives the answer 49?

19 If I save 20p a day from Wednesday until Saturday,
how much will I have?

20 Mary picked 5 kilograms of apples. Neeta picked
3 kilograms more than Mary. How many did
they pick altogether?

The **Long** and the **short**

Which is the longest line in each row, A, B or C?

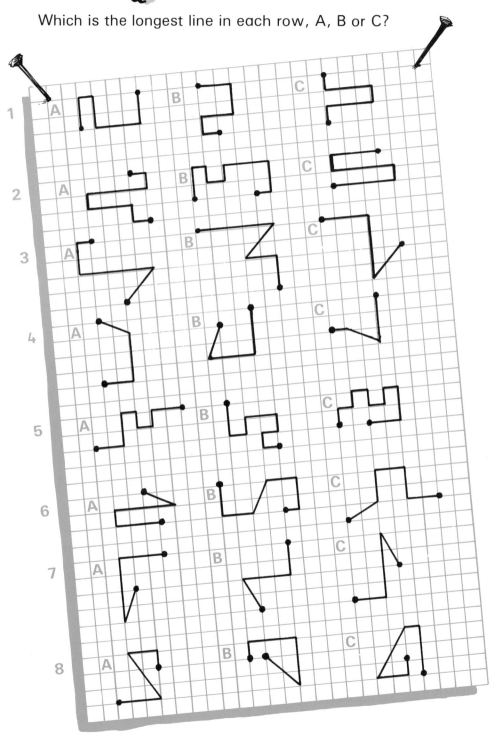

Task 15

A

1 What is the sum of fifteen and 15?

2 From twenty-six take eleven.

3 Find five lots of 9.

4 How many children can each be given 4 sweets if I share out 24 sweets?

5 Peter had eighteen conkers, but then seven were beaten. How many had he left?

6 Multiply 65 by 10.

7 Put these in order, smallest first: 47, 39, 58, 36.

8 340 ÷ 10.

9 What is the value of the two in 249?

10 What is the smallest number that can be made using

B

11 What is the next number? 22, 19, 16, 13, ?

12 Is 50 centimetres + 40 centimetres > 1 metre?

13 What is half of 60?

14 Is 5:40 the same as twenty to six?

15 Does my car hold 30 litres or 30 millilitres of petrol in its tank?

16 Pencils cost 8p each, and rubbers cost 6p. How much will it cost for 3 pencils and 2 rubbers?

17 3 apples cost 20p. How much will 9 apples cost?

18 25 bottles fill a crate. How many bottles are there in 4 full crates?

19 Paula arrived at the bus stop at a quarter past four. The bus came ten minutes later. When did it arrive?

20 If four times a number is 36, what is twice that number?

Task 16

1   Find the total of 38 and eleven.

2   Twenty-seven take away nine.

3   How many shoes would sixteen children wear?

4   Mr Miles is putting 4 wheels onto each soap box. How many soap boxes can be fitted with 28 wheels?

5   Mum made twelve buns. Andrew ate three. How many were left?

6   How far from the nearest ten is 106?

7   Take 10 from 308.

8   Divide 410 by 10.

9   Which two of these numbers add up to ten?   3,   8,   9,   2,   6.

10   What is the value of the three in 103?

11   Is ¼ of an hour > twenty minutes?

12   Is 36 a multiple of three?

13   What is double twenty-six?

14   How many days were there in February 1985?

15   What is the next number?   6,   10,   14,   18,   ?

16   The bus had 25 passengers. At the next stop 8 people got on and 3 got off. How many passengers were there now?

17   I buy two apples costing 8p each. What change do I get from 50p?

18   Megan is a quarter of her Dad's age. If she is ten, how old is her Dad?

19   Anne has 12p, and Mark has 18p. If they share their money, how much will they each get?

20   What number when multiplied by two gives eighty as the answer?

20

Task 17

1 What is twelve more than 24?

2 Take eight from 22.

3 Daniel, Christopher and Tina each have nine conkers. How many do they have altogether?

4 Mum is putting 4 sandwiches on a plate. How many plates can she fill with thirty-two sandwiches?

5 Cub Scouts line up in six rows of six. How many of them are there?

6 What number is one less than 140?

7 72×10.

8 Add 10 to the largest number here: 42, 27, 56, 38, 47.

9 Write **516** in words.

10 How far from the nearest ten is 198?

11 How many grams are there in a ¼ of a kilogram?

12 What is a quarter of 24?

13 Is 65p + 35p > £1?

14 Is it 50 centimetres or 50 metres around Sue's waist?

15 If today is Thursday, which day was it 6 days' ago?

16 Toffees cost 7p each, and sherbets cost 8p. How much will 3 toffees and 2 sherbets cost?

17 What number is halfway between 32 and 40?

18 I have seven 5p coins. If I spend 22p, how much will I have left?

19 Philip has 30 marbles, but Pat has 15 more than him. How many have they altogether?

20 How long is it from ten minutes to five until 5:15?

One shape in each row is not finished.
Copy out and complete the missing one from each row.

Task 18

A

1 Add thirteen to twenty.

2 Take sixteen from 28.

3 Five children each have seven sweets.
How many sweets is that altogether?

4 Share 32 by 4.

5 Six children sit at a table.
If there are five full tables, how many children are there?

6 Put these in order, smallest first: 87, 103, 29, 83.

7 Add 100 to 146.

8 How many tens are there in 390?

9 What number is one more than 189?

10 What is the value of the seven in 179?

11 Is 30p + 40p + 50p < £1?

12 Does tea come in packets of 500 grams or 500 kilograms?

13 Is 36 a multiple of 4?

> Multiples of four
> 4, 8, 12, 16, 20

14 What is twice the sum of 7 and 8?

15 How many days are there in November?

> 24

16 If I save 20p every day for a week, how much
will I have saved at the end?

> 28

17 Hitesh has 20p, and Grace has 8p. If they share
their money, how much will they each get?

18 Rosie arrived for the bus at 10:20. It came at 10:35.
How long did Rosie wait?

19 Peter has walked 5 kilometres, but he still has
twice as far again to go. How long is his journey altogether?

20 4 toffees cost 10p. How much do 12 toffees cost?

Task 19

1 What is the total of sixteen and sixteen?

2 What is nine less than 22?

3 Find 3×8.

4 Chocolate biscuits are packed 5 to a box.
How many boxes can be filled with twenty-five biscuits?

5 Charlie has twenty-six stamps. If he sells seven,
how many will he have left?

6 What number is one less than 200?

7 What is the value of the one in 712?

8 $380 \div 10$.

9 Add ten to the largest number here: 41, 39, 52, 28, 47.

10 Which two of these numbers add up to 20?
13, 8, 16, 7, 2.

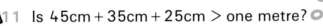

Write cm
for centimetres

11 Is $45cm + 35cm + 25cm$ > one metre?

12 What is the next number?   29, 25, 21, 17, ?

13 Are my fingers 7 cm or 7 metres long?

14 Is half an hour < twenty minutes?

15 Is this
7:55?

16 How long is it from 5 minutes to 9 until 9:30?

17 The bus had 30 passengers, then 9 people got off
while 12 people got on. How many were on the bus now?

18 If I buy five 8p lemons, what change will I get from £1?

19 David took 40 conkers to school. Sally took 10 more
than David. How many did they have altogether?

20 I have nine 5p coins. If I spent 28p, how much will I have left?

24

Task 20

A

1   Add together eighteen and twelve.

2   28 − 17.

3   Find nine lots of three.

4   A box of thirty oranges is used to fill 5 bags.
    How many oranges will there be in each bag?

5   Grace has 26 pencil crayons, but seven need
    sharpening. How many can she use now?

6   Take 100 from 506.

7   Write **two hundred and ninety-six** in figures.

8   How many tens are there in 297?

9   What is the largest number that can be made using

10   Write these in order, largest first: 40,   93,   107,   56.

B

11   What is a quarter of 28?

12   How many days are there in four weeks?

13   How many days are there in June?

14   What is double the sum of 9 and 6?

15   Is 6:45 the same as a quarter to six?

16   4 chocolate sweets cost 15p.
     How much do 16 chocolate sweets cost?

17   What number when divided by six gives the answer 7?

18   20 bottles fill a crate.
     How many crates can I fill with 100 bottles?

19   Davina arrived at 9:05 for the twenty past nine bus.
     How long did she have to wait?

20   Pears cost 7p each. How much change will I get
     from 30p after buying 4 pears?

Task 21

1 What is eighteen more than twenty-two?

2 Take 16 from 24.

3 Mum, Dad and Uncle Arthur each eat four sandwiches. How many do they eat altogether?

4 Granny is sewing four buttons on each cardigan. How many cardigans can she fit with 12 buttons?

5 What are six lots of nine ?

6 How far from the nearest ten is 316?

7 Multiply 42 by 10.

8 Write **two hundred and eighteen** in figures.

9 Add ten to the smallest number here: 48, 106, 39, 54, 88.

10 What number is one less than 350?

11 Does an apple weigh 100 grams or 100 kilograms?

12 How many grams are there in ¾ of a kilogram?

13 Is $5 \times 5 < 4 \times 6$?

14 Is 40 a multiple of 5?

15 If today is Thursday, how many days ago was last Sunday?

16 What number is halfway between 19 and 25?

17 Chrissie gives Mark half of her sweets. If she started with 12 sweets, how many has she now?

18 If March 4th is a Wednesday, on which day is March 8th?

19 Dad gives Tim 20p a week pocket money. If he saves all of it, how long would it take Tim to save £1?

20 Pencils cost 9p each, and rubbers cost 7p. How much would 2 pencils and 4 rubbers cost?

Deca-enlarger

This machine adds two numbers and then multiplies the answer by ten. Do the same for each sum. Remember to multiply by 10.

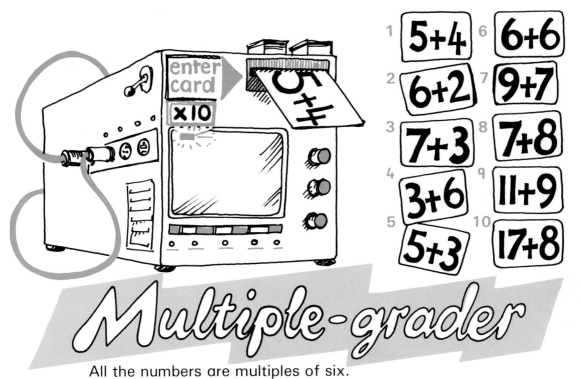

1	5+4	6	6+6
2	6+2	7	9+7
3	7+3	8	7+8
4	3+6	9	11+9
5	5+3	10	17+8

Multiple-grader

All the numbers are multiples of six.
This machine divides each one in turn by 6.
You try to do the same.

1	18	6	60
2	48	7	54
3	36	8	42
4	24	9	72
5	30	10	120

48

enter card

÷6

Task 22

A

1   Add thirteen to seventeen.

2   What is twenty-three take away eight?

3   Nicola, Helen and Samuel each have five coloured pencils. How many have they altogether?

4   Divide 27 by 3.

5   Share 26 marbles between Sue and Phil. How many do they each get?

6   How many tens are there in 420?

7   Add 100 to 207.

8   Write these in order, smallest first: 48,   39,   107,   53.

9   Which two of these numbers add up to 20? 12,   3,   14,   8,   7.

10   What is the value of the two in 203?

B

11   Is the road in which I live 180 metres or 180 kilometres long?

12   Is 40p + 30p + 20p > £1?

13   What is the time here?

14   What is the next number?   19,   16,   13,   ?

15   What is a quarter of 32?

16   What number when divided by 6 gives the answer 9?

17   The bus had 32 people on it. 8 got off while 9 got on. How many were now on the bus?

18   What change do I get from 50p after buying six 6p toffees?

19   Chris waited a quarter of an hour for the bus, which arrived at ten minutes past four. When did Chris start waiting?

20   I have two 10p coins and five 5p coins. How much more do I need to have 50p?

Task 23

A

1 Find the total of twenty-six and fourteen.

2 Take seventeen from 29.

3 Multiply 7 by 6.

4 Mr Harvey needs teams of six. He has eighteen children in his class. How many teams can be make?

5 Deena has 15 apples and she eats three a day.
How many days will they last?

6 Divide 450 by ten.

7 Find 65 lots of ten.

8 Write these in order, largest first: 87, 107, 119, 92.

9 What is the smallest number that can be made using

10 How far from the nearest ten is 208?

B

11 Is a tree 10 m tall or 100 m tall?

12 Is 300 grams + 400 grams < one kilogram?

13 Is twenty to eight the same as 8:20?

14 If today is Tuesday, how many days will it be until next Saturday?

15 What is the time?

Metres is written m for short

16 Apples cost 9p each. How much change will I get from 50p after buying 2 apples?

17 How long is it from ten minutes to eight until 8:25?

18 If it takes 20 minutes to walk 2 kilometres, how long would it take to walk 6 kilometres?

19 If 3 oranges cost 20p, how many would I get for £1?

20 What number when divided by 7 gives the answer 7?

Task 24

1 Add fifteen to twelve.

2 30 − 17.

3 Find four lots of seven.

4 Share 25 biscuits among five children.
   How many do they each get?

5 Melanie likes chocolate buttons. If she eats 5 a day,
   how many will she eat in a week?

6 Take 100 from 463.

7 Add 10 to the smallest number here: 48,   33,   59,   71.

8 Write **405** in words.

9 What is the value of the six in the number 406?

10 Which two of these numbers add up to twenty?
   2,   8,   17,   14,   3.

11 Does a man weigh 7 kg or 70 kg?

> For kilograms write **kg** for short

12 Is 300 grams > ¼ of a kilogram?

13 Is 5 weeks < 1 month?

14 How many weeks are there in ½ a year?

15 What time is it?

16 I have one 50p coin, two 10p coins and three 5p coins.
   How much more do I need to have £1?

17 What number is halfway between 33 and 39?

18 Graham was 15 minutes early for his bus.
   He arrived at 11:55. When did the bus come?

19 35 people started on the bus. If 11 got on while 9 got off,
   how many are on the bus now?

20 Two packets of jelly weigh 300g. What does one
   packet weigh?

Cat Hoop-la

1 The picture shows Colin's score for Cat Hoop-La.
   What was the total score for all the rings?

2 Patricia got two rings on number 7, and one each on
   9 and 11. What was her total score?

3 One boy scored 35 with three rings.
   Which numbers did he get?

4 Susan scored 9, 6 and 15. What was her total score?

5 Which of these numbers cannot be scored with only
   two hoops on the Cat Hoop-la? 16, 17, 18, 19.

6 Find three different ways of scoring 40.

7 How many is four lots of 15?

8 Is it possible to score 44 with 5 rings?

9 Is it possible to score 54 with 5 rings?

10 Is it possible to score 64 with 5 rings?

Task 25

A

1   Find the sum of seventeen and thirteen.

2   What are six lots of eight?

3   If bananas are 7p each, how much would six cost?

4   A florist had 48 roses.
    How many bunches of six roses could she make?

5   Take nine from twenty-five.

6   Write **two hundred and forty-six** in figures.

7   Multiply 63 by 10.

8   What is ten less than 447?

9   What is the value of the six in 406?

10 Add 10 to the smallest number here: 49, 37, 24, 83, 72.

B

11 What is the next number?   14,   11,   8,   ?

12 Is 27 a multiple of 3?

13 How many minutes are there in 2 hours?

For grams write g for short

14 Does 350 g + 750 g weigh more than one kilogram?

15 What is the least number of coins needed to make 23p?

16 Tea and biscuits cost 25p.
    How much will it be for 4 people?

17 Pencils cost 6p each, and rubbers cost 5p.
    How much will 2 rubbers and 3 pencils cost?

18 Find the total value of three 2p coins,
    six 5p coins and one 20p coin.

19 What is twice the sum of 7 and fifteen?

20 How many 200 gram packets can be made from
    one kilogram of sugar?

Task 26

1. Add together five, nine and 16.

2. What is the difference between eight and twenty-three?

3. Find five lots of seven.

4. How many groups of four can be made from twenty?

5. How much will three cups of tea cost at 8p a cup?

6. Which number comes just before 207?

7. Divide 130 by 10.

8. Add ten to 529.

9. How many pennies are there in £1.37?

10. Write **311** in words.

11. Is 47 a multiple of 5?

12. Could a baby weigh 90 kilograms?

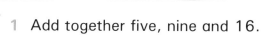

½ turn

W

13. If I face west and make a half turn, in which direction will I face?

A factor divides without a remainder

14. Is 2 a factor of 10?

15. How many 5p coins are needed to make 65p?

16. Pencils cost 9p each. How much change will I get from £1 after buying 6 pencils?

17. How many days are there altogether in July and August?

18. It is 240 kilometres from here to Irkham. How far is it there and back?

19. If June 3rd is a Wednesday, on which day is June 9th?

20. If I cut 75 cm from a metre plank, how many centimetres are left?

Task 27

A

1. What is the total of eighteen and twenty-two?

2. From twenty-six take seven.

3. Hina buys 5 pencils which cost 9p each.
   How much does she spend?

4. Share 15 by three.

5. Find four lots of eight.

6. Write **five hundred and sixty-seven** in figures.

7. Multiply 72 by 10.

8. What is ten more than 497?

9. What is the value of the seven in 709?

10. Take ten from the smallest number
    here: 111, 107, 117, 170, 127.

A full turn

B

11. What is the next number?   17,   13,   9,   5,   ?

12. Is 24 a multiple of 4?

13. How many right-angles are there in a full turn?

14. How long is it from 7:15 until 8:00?

15. Does 10 cm + 40 cm + 50 cm make a metre?

16. 8 nails weigh 60 grams. What do 24 similar nails weigh?

17. If a man walks at 6 kilometres an hour,
    how long will it take him to walk 15 kilometres?

18. How many days is it from July 25th until August 8th?

19. David has 16p, and Maria has 8p. If they share their
    money, how much will they each get?

20. Three pears cost 20p. How many pears could I buy
    with 60p?

Task 28

A

1 How much is nine more than twenty-one?

2 What is fourteen less than 21?

3 John has 25p pocket money. If a comic cost him 13p, how much has he left?

4 Apples are 6p each. How many can I buy with 30p?

5 Multiply seven by 6.

6 Take 20 from 127.

7 Divide 210 by 10.

8 Add ten to 397.

9 How many pennies are there in £9.46?

10 Write **616** in words.

11 Is 32 a multiple of three?

12 What is the time?

13 How many centimetres are there in half a metre?

14 Is 4 a factor of 12?

15 What is the least number of coins needed to make 42p?

16 If coffee cost 20p and cake cost 15p, how much is 3 coffees and 2 cakes?

17 What is the average of 3, 10 and 5?

18 How long is it from 10:30 a.m. until 11:15 a.m.?

19 How many ½ kilogram packets can be made from 5 kilograms of sugar?

20 Apples cost 11p each. How many can I buy with £1? What change do I get?

To find the average of three numbers, add them together and then divide by 3

A page of pets

1 How many children have a cat?

2 Who has only one pet?

3 How many children own a dog?

4 How many pets are owned by these children altogether?

5 What can you say about Jonathan?

6 How many pet rabbits are there?

7 How many more dogs are owned by the children than rabbits?

8 Who has most pets?

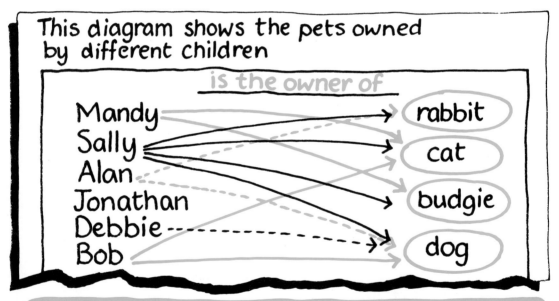

This diagram shows the pets owned by different children

is the owner of

Mandy	rabbit
Sally	cat
Alan	budgie
Jonathan	dog
Debbie	
Bob	

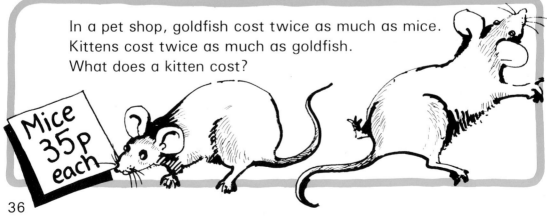

In a pet shop, goldfish cost twice as much as mice.
Kittens cost twice as much as goldfish.
What does a kitten cost?

Mice 35p each

Task 29

A

1 What is the answer to fifteen add sixteen?

2 Take nineteen from twenty-six.

3 Find eight lots of 5.

4 If a pear costs 9p, how much will four pears cost?

5 Pencils cost 8p each. How many can I buy with 32p?

6 Write **five hundred and two** in figures.

7 Multiply 47 by 10.

8 What is ten less than 809?

9 What is the value of the eight in 811?

10 Take 100 from the largest number
here: 107,   192,   174,   127.

B

11 What is the next number?   3,   10,   17,   24,   ?

12 Is 28 a multiple of 4?

13 Could Robert easily lift 500 grams or 500 kilograms?

14 How much is ¼ of £1?

15 What is
the time?

16 How many days are there in October and
November altogether?

17 Jane cuts two ribbons each 33 centimetres long
from a metre length. How much is left?

18 Bill cycles at 12 kilometres an hour for 1 ½ hours.
How far does he cycle?

19 If his journey of 1 ½ hours starts at 10:15,
when does it end?

20 Find the cost of ten 15p stamps.

Task 30

A

1   Add nine to fifteen.

2   What is the difference between seventeen and 29?

3   How much change is there from 50p after buying a pen for 23p?

4   Share 27 by 9.

5   Find six lots of eight.

6   Take ten from 208.

7   Divide 460 by ten.

8   Add ten to 497.

9   How many pennies are there in £1.67?

10 Write **774** in words.

B

11 Is 25 a multiple of 4?

12 Is 3 a factor of 10?

13 How tall is Joanne if she is 13 centimetres taller than a metre?

14 How many grams are there in 1 ½ kilograms?

15 How long is it from 6:30 p.m. until 7:15 p.m.?

16 What is the average of 4, 6 and 11?

17 Lorna is twice as old as Peter.
    If their ages add up to 9 years, how old is Peter?

18 What is the cost of three books at 55p each?

19 If a snail crawls 10 centimetres in 10 minutes, how far will it crawl in an hour?

20 A cook fried 24 fish fingers.
    How many people could each have three of these?

38